Johann Wentzel
20 Windsor Lodge
Waringstown
BT66 7GS
Tel: (44) 078 5041 7675
Johann.Wentzel@BTinternet.com

Also by Johann Wentzel

Are they the same size?

Emails from Ireland

Where is my Tickey?

I have found my Tickey

(Afrikaans)

Waar is my Tiekie?

Ek het my Tiekie gevind

suiderkruis karos

The Schizophrenia of JC

Johann Wentzel

Johann Wentzel was born in South Africa on the 24th of August 1952 but he grew up in South-West Africa now called Namibia. Johann is the eldest of four children and himself the father of three, a son and two daughters. He is a computer programmer, married to Linda and has been living in Co. Armagh, Northern Ireland since July 2006.

www.JohannWentzel.com

amazon.com/author/johann.wentzel

For Linda

Chapter 1

I was standing on top of the reservoir. I was thirsty and there was no need for me to climb to the top of the stark concrete structure. It did not take a genius to know that it will be impossible to get to the water. I knew that even before I started the trek up the mountain to the reservoir.

Schizophrenia makes you vulnerable. Taking medication for it make the people around you vulnerable. It is like a broken tooth. Your tongue keeps on going back to explore the cavity. Keeps on going back to be ripped but it has a will of its own. It is the same with schizophrenia. It circles like a leopard sniffing at the door posts; leaving its mark. Circling and circling ever closer but impossible to see. Impossible to know when it will make its silent killer move.

It was hot in the midday sun on top of the reservoir but the rough concrete was strangely cool under my bare feet. There was dry blood on my right big toe where the nail was pushed back during my climb up the mountain.

It wasn't really a mountain. More like a hill but still high enough to ensure a good water flow to the houses down at the foot of the rocky outcrop. The reservoir would sometimes run dry towards the end of an extra-long winter. You get used to that. One gets used to anything; even waiting for rain.

I could see the whole world stretching out before me. I could hold it in the palm of my hand. I should have stayed in the bit of man-made shade at the bottom of the reservoir or I should have started back immediately while I still had the strength, but it was there and I was close, so close. I could not help myself. I reached forward to pick it up. To protect it as it has protected me. That is what the voice said. That it is yours for the taking. I had to do it. It was destined for me.

My brother Jonathan was looking down at me when I opened my eyes. He was smiling. Pleased to see me. I was a day old. I should never have started smoking. He should never have married her. These two things drove us apart. That and then the child. The child. His child. How can I say it? How can I even think it? How can I blame a severely handicapped child with bright smiley soul blue eyes? Blue eyes like my dad, like me. A broken child with my dad's names and mine. God forgive me.

I should never have been born. My dad should never have filed for bankruptcy. We should never have moved. I should never have gone to the army. People should have called me James, not Jim.

They should have left me at the bottom of the reservoir or I should have missed the dense scrubs that cushioned my fall and rather have ended up head first on the black burned rocks, or the water board's maintenance team should have scheduled another day, but sometimes the universe has other plans.

Chapter 2

Narcissistic according to the first psychologist and I had no problem with that. That was until I researched narcissism further!

Then the label changed to schizophrenic after being seen by the first physiatrist, at which point I have lost interest, but I did mention I can't help thinking that I am in two minds about this one. (It was a repetitive joke that raised a few smiles every time.) This all only came to be many years later; two thousand years later when it was no longer the done thing to send pigs avalanching over a cliff.

Test results, any test result is a bit like death. The test itself becomes meaningless as the result takes on a life of its own. Death only becomes a reality after the second death; when the last person that remembers your name dies.

I will therefore never die. I will only cease to exist when the sun has burned out after swallowing Earth and when the universe implodes into itself and the next big bang spews out the new universe and then I will return for ever and ever, like my recurring dream.

I am before you were and I will be long after you have been and I will cycle in and through you in despair and pain again and again. My burden will become your burden. My longing your longing. The weight of my recurring dream will keep you from ever sleeping again.

It is finished.

Chapter 3

I was thirty three when I died the first time. I died a horrible death with my hands tied above my head and in my death my dream returned but this time I did not wake up. I was awake and there were no distractions. My dream became reality as it finally fell into place, taking me back to my own inception. Some experiences are worse than death.

Maryam, my mother was a young mother. Her too-early pregnancy with me forced her body into premature womanhood. I could never forgive myself for that. She never blamed me. She should have but there are certain crimes that no punishment will do justice.

She was quickly married off to a man in another village and never saw her family again. She died more than once. I did not grow up in the town or even county where I was born.

My bought father was a simple man but quick enough to accept payment to cover her family's shame. I cannot recall the first time when I had my dream but it was long after the money had run out.

My mother was sitting on the wall of the well running her fingers through her hair, waiting for her turn to draw water for the house. They had servants but she wanted to go with. She convinced her parents that it was safe. She was a pretty girl and could twist her father around her little finger even in a time when daughters were worth far less than sons.

Our country is a dry country. Certain life truths don't have to be taught. Children grow up knowing to treasure water. I formulated a few truths myself. It is a miracle for coping when the thoughts become too much. It is playing your own motion picture with only you in the audience. It is growing up with siblings that are not like you. Not when you are your mother's favourite. Not when you know you cannot possibly be like them. There are certain things that you just know. That you know even before the voice speaks the first time.

It was the thirst that nearly killed me that allowed me to hear the voice clearly for the first time. It never left again. The voice was me and I was the voice. It happened when I got lost in the dry riverbed outside town and instead of turning around and going home, I climbed to the top of the reservoir that supplied water to all the houses down in the flat, dry, windless valley. It was the view across the barren land dancing in the mirage of the midday sun that brought the first vision. I was destined for greater things. I just knew it, even before the voice confirmed it. It was my unplanned birthright. I did not need a book to confirm it, even though I did find it in a book.

I started school when I was six. I was bored at school. I already knew everything. I learned quickly not to let on what I knew. I read more and more. Anything with printed words that I could lay my hands on, even the plastic bottles in the school toilet sitting on a toilet without a lid or toilet paper on the roll. I was sitting amongst elders from centuries gone.

I knew early on that any page in any book can answer any question. Just think about your question really hard, open the book in your hand on any page and start reading where your eyes first focus. The answer will be there. We are each a god in our own right. It was my duty to show that to the world.

I thirst.

Chapter 4

My mother was sitting on the bench next to the stream when she dropped her guard. She was so innocent. She took her golden scarf from her head and shook her head ever so slightly as not to attract attention. Her dark hair tumbled down her back and that caught his eyes. The eyes of Leopard. Paths cross as determined by the universe.

Always water, always waiting, always the danger softly lurking just outside view. Always just outside the vision of my dream but I would always wake up, heart racing with a dry month, like a dog with rabies too scared of water to go for a drink in the middle of the night but knowing that the dream was necessary. That I have to dream it again. To concentrate in my dream to not wake up but to live it to the end. To save me and so to save the world. That my dream is the only real thing in my world.

I don't know whether I screamed when I had my dream the first time but my mother was there as I opened my eyes. Holding me, soothing me, telling me it was only a dream. It was only after the fourth or fifth time that I noticed her own tears. I forced myself to not scream when dreaming, but she knew. She would just be there, soothing and softly telling me I am special. That I will always be special. It was only later that she became the child and I the parent. That was good. No parent should lose a child. Children should bury their parents.

Behold your son: behold your mother.

Chapter 5

Knowing everything does not mean understanding everything. How can one ask for forgiveness for something that you did not do? For something that you are the result of but not the reason for? How can one break the circle that runs through your mind? Questions with no answer but questions never the less. Questions that drive you into the desert to get you away from yourself just to confront yourself.

How did I know that I had a father? Not the one that was the father of my brothers and sisters but a real father? I always knew that. It came to me in my mother's midnight tears mingling with mine. My dream her dream. It was her Leopard in a Roman tunic; Dante's Inferno. I was her constant companion. I had to complete the final stage on my own: nine circles of suffering. It took three days; half the time it took my father to create the universe.

We are all one. There is no time but that measured by man. One of our inventions to cope within the universe. I breathe your breath. If not now then in a million years from now or a million years ago. I share your pain until it becomes too much for one and then I pass it on. We recycle, caught in the trap of being human. No, that is what being human is.

Freud always knew he had a father. He never doubted that even though he felt betrayed by him. Certain things are burned into your being for ever and ever. Freud's libido was awaken by seeing his mother naked while travelling on a train when he was two and a half years old. He, Freud only lost his virginity when he got married at age thirty.

The universe has a sense of humour. He was afraid to travel on trains for the rest of his life.

My mother lost her virginity against her will, taken by Leopard at age nearly thirteen. It cost her her family. She poured her pain and her loss into her son. He had no way out. She did not allow him a way out. He had to take responsibility as best he could. It caused his name to be used to destroy millions of lives. It was schizophrenia never documented or rather documented in so much detail that it got lost.

My God, my God, why have you forsaken me?

Chapter 6

Schizophrenia wears different jackets. Some with ties others without. It seems to be ashamed of itself; calling itself by different names, hiding in the dark but ready to pounce when least expected. It is a world that could have been invented by Dante. It pulls you down and delivers you to your own demons.

I Googled it – many times. In the middle of the night. In the middle of the day. Typed schizophrenia without thinking. Hitting the enter button without being aware of it but I had to read all the definitions every time. Every time without fail even when I was silently screaming, clutching at my head, willing the voice to just once not interrupt. I could see myself, holding my scream, looking like *The Scream*. Silently scaring people while attracting them in open mouth horror.

It scares people for a million different reasons. People are selfish. Some are afraid that it is contagious and that they may attract it or that they may have to admit that they already have it. That they themselves are infected. We all are. We all have the seed of it in us. We all pat our pockets to make sure we have our keys when leaving the house. We all think that the oven may be on, rattle the door knob knowing that it was locked moments ago. We all shift the blame.

Schizophrenia is in the basic blueprint of being human. Embedded in our genes. It is just not as developed in everybody and we all know that. We are all afraid of the shadow circling just outside the reach of the fire at night while we huddle together, too afraid to investigate. Too afraid to explore inwards. Too afraid of what we may unleash. For once it is set free it can never be contained again. We all know that.

I knew that even after I stole my psychiatric records and hid the then still, slim folder under the loose carpet in my brother, Jonathan's bedroom. I felt guilty and phoned him to tell him where it was even before the mental institution realised it was missing. That is part of the disease. The never ending feelings of guilt. Of fear, of anxiety, of paranoia. Of not knowing what is going to happen next. Of not being in control. Of being bored for no reason. Of burning yourself on your forehead with a cigarette just to see whether you can get rid of your third eye. Of hurting those closest to you without being able to stop. Of crying with those that cry for you.

Jonathan returned the file. It grew much bigger over time as more and more pages were added. As more and more tests were done. As more and more drugs were prescribed.

I will finally die when my brother stops crying.

Chapter 7

Do we forgive the lessor evil for the greater good? Or is forgiveness only possible when it does not impact me directly? Or because the evil was done many moons ago before I was born?

It is said by them, those faceless like the public service or those that dream up health and safety rules, that: "Narcissism is a severe psychological disorder that always takes root in childhood, where family life is marked by trauma and emotional chaos. Blah, blah, blah. When his or her earliest experiences drastically depart from what is normal or expectable, the child grows up with a painful feeling of internal defect. Blah, blah, blah. He or she comes to feel that there is something damaged and shameful about himself or herself, an "ugliness" that must be concealed. He or she may grow up feeling that he or she is a "loser." And so he or she develops a defensive identity to hide his or her unconscious shame and to "prove" that he or she is a winner instead. Blah, blah, blah"

But what do they know, sitting in their ivory towers? Think! What about Leonardo da Vinci? He was illegitimate and his mom was also married off by his biological father to a local man of lesser standing. His mother who then refused to treat him as her son while going on to have many more. Is he remembered firstly as a narcissist or as a painter scientist genius? Do they have a collective feeling of guilt because he was prevented from enrolling at a university because he was born a bastard?

Leonardo da Vinci wrote "learning never exhausts the mind." That may be true but I will add, "Learning also does not explain the mind". Not when your mind forces you to live inwards. When it forces you to look inwards.

And what about the great, cigar chain-smoking, Sigmund Freud? He felt betrayed by his father after his father went bankrupt when his wool business failed and when his father, even then, could not hold down a steady job. Is he remembered as the man that wanted to kill his father so that he could sleep with his mother?

Do they, the faceless, change or invent labels to appease themselves?

Are we born to believe or do we embrace religion because it encourages us to cast the first stone? Or to stop us from seeing? The complete opposite of da Vinci's *saper vedere,* "knowing how to see"?

Can ignorance only be washed away by blood?

Chapter 8

I was a wanted child, the youngest of four and much younger than the other three. Wanted in the sense that my mother was suffering from empty nest syndrome according to the doctor. Rather a baby than anti-depressants, he said.

My eldest brother Jonathan took over when my mother lost interest. It is not fair to her to say "lost interest". It is more a case of not knowing where to next. Not knowing what to expect next. I am so sorry. So sorry for so many things and to so many people. I should never have started smoking. My brother hated that and it drove us apart. More so than my disease. I am so sorry.

That is the main problem of my so called disease. It weighs up every possible impact. Every single current and future outcome that may hurt someone somewhere sometime. It becomes too much. I become the sole guardian of the world every split second of every waking minute and in my dreams as well. I am so sorry. I am so sorry that I have to protect myself. That I have to co-exist with and within myself. That I had to get out and stand on the top of the car in the hospital car park while my brother was completing the paperwork for me to be admitted to the psychiatric ward on the third floor. But it was good how I manipulated the security guards into praying with me afterwards while waiting in their office. Praying for them after I told them to hold hands and close their eyes. I am getting ahead of myself, but I have an excuse; a normal timeline is not the trademark of a schizophrenic. My timeline is pockmarked by what the voice tells me.

I am lucky; my voice has no name. My voice is just me knowing. My voice does not talk to me, is not god. My voice is me, is me, me!

I was a planned child and I got my father's names. All four his names.

I never got love when I needed it.

Chapter 9

I left my own five year old self in Windhoek that day when we left Namibia for Johannesburg in South Africa. I waved at my own self standing lost in the driveway of the empty house as the car turned around the corner. I was lost. I had nowhere to go, no home and I was five years old.

I could already count. Jonathan taught me to count before I could even talk. I found myself again in numbers and I knew. I have always known that the answer is never the same except when proven in numbers.

I was in a car piled high with all our worldly possessions and I was counting. I counted the telephone poles as they come closer from far away. Small to grow bigger only to silently fly past just to disappear in the streak of dust behind the car; only the next number in the one-way travelling game of a bored five year old child.

I counted telephone poles on and off for twenty hours; for just over a thousand miles: thousands and thousands of knotted wooden telephone poles carrying millions and millions of messages in both directions all over the world and I knew then that there is no beginning and no end. I knew then that there is another universe where I did not have to leave Windhoek. A universe where my dad did not lose everything. A universe where we did not have to start over again. A universe where someone cared for me.

I had to say goodbye to myself again when I was twelve years old and Jonathan's son was born. Had to leave that universe and then again at thirteen when Lovey died. It never stopped; again when Dorothy left, when Johanna left, when my mom died. It never stopped or went away. I knew then that each universe that I leave behind will come back. That every loss will spawn a new start. That it will always be there to reach out and punish me. I knew then that I will have to live in multiple universes as my thoughts dictate.

I had no choice. I had to learn to live with my fear as best as I could under all circumstances.

I also had to learn that not everybody can understand that our universe is but a knot in a telephone post on the dusty road of the cosmos. That this solar system is but one cell in a larger body, a larger body that in turn is but a cell in one of the knots in the next telephone post. Like the red-and-white picture of the Royal yeast tin in the red-and-white picture of the Royal yeast tin... Like the uncountable cells in our bodies, every cell a solar system controlled by the same simple laws. Like the uncountable worlds in every teardrop that people have shed for me and I am sorry. I am so sorry but I had to protect myself in the only way I knew. I had many universes to take care of and nobody to take care of me. I am so sorry. I really am.

Chapter 10

We moved into a round single roomed thatched rondavel on a farm about twenty miles from the nearest town. It was quick to settle in. We, as a family had no material possessions. My poor mother. Poverty imposes its own difficulties but it did allow me to withdraw into my own private world. I did not need love. I knew that. Jonathan once again went off to boarding school. I was once again left on my own. I had time to explore. The answers came quicker than what I could process.

I realised that time, as money is man-made with no foundation in logic. That time measures distance in a never ending circle in an attempt to keep us grounded. To force us to live and relive only the now. That all of us are one enslaved. That we will meet ourselves again and again. That time was a feeble attempt to give purpose and direction in a singular world.

I realised that religion was at best an attempt to allow us to start again. To escape the pain that will come back again and again. That there is only hope. That The Bible is wrong in saying that love is the greatest of these three: faith, hope, love. We can live without love. There is only hope.

The rondavel had an outside toilet and bathroom. It also had a hard smooth floor finished with a mixture of dung and mud. I had to make my own way in the middle of the night. I was five years old and I missed my brother. I could look up into the cloudless night sky and I could lose myself to find myself. I could wait. Jonathan would be back. He will never leave me.

I was really excited. We were on our way into town. It was a Friday afternoon and schools were breaking up for the long six week December holidays. We were on our way to pick my brothers up from boarding school.

I went with Jonathan into his dorm room to get all his luggage. He would not come back the next year. He would have to go to the Army. He would go to the Army and it was time for me to start big school the next year in January, just after Christmas. But first I had to go to the toilet. I was so excited when we left home that I forgot to go to the toilet. Jonathan just laughed and took me to the big boys' toilet.

Jonathan and I had to stand next to one another to pee into the long stainless steel urinal that ran the whole length of the one wall in their big bathroom. Jonathan was telling me that girls don't stand when they go for a wee. Girls had to sit down. I felt really big standing next to my big brother and peeing into the same trough. That is what Jonathan called it; a "trough" like the pigs on the farm eat from. I never sat down on the toilet seat ever again after that when I only wanted to make a pee. I peed into the water standing so that everybody could hear it was a boy in the toilet and not a girl. Jonathan called it doing a number "one".

Jonathan also told me that he had a girlfriend. Her name was Anne. He told me first so I already knew when he told my mom and dad in the car on the way back to the farm. We all laughed and my dad said: "Congratulations and when will we meet her?"

I was also the first one to meet Jonathan's girlfriend Anne. He and I went to visit her just before Christmas and Jonathan gave her a ring with a pearl in it. She was so excited that she grabbed him and gave him lots of kisses. He turned all red and couldn't talk. Especially when Anne's mom walked into the room. I stood up when Anne's mom entered the room. Jonathan taught me that. One always has to get up when a girl or a woman enters a room. Anne's mom also laughed and gave me a kiss. I really liked Anne. She would always asked me how I was and called me Jamie when I was the first to answer the phone when she would phone looking for Jonathan. I didn't mind that. I liked it. Jamie was the same as being called James.

Chapter 11

Jonathan gave me a brass boiler steam engine that Christmas. One had to make a small fire with special dry fuel to get it to build up steam to turn the little flywheel and driving pulley. It even had a steam-powered whistle. I was technically still too young to operate it by myself, as it was intended for children older than eight under adult supervision, but Jonathan said I was cleverest little boy in the world and I believed him. I believed everything that he said. Jonathan was my only ever hero: Jonathan and Isaac Newton. I kept the little steam engine my whole life. It was my one single most precious possession. I also knew that Jonathan wanted one his whole life. He never had his own one but we often played together with mine.

Jonathan must have saved all his money that he earned doing odd jobs that year to buy Anne and my Christmas presents. Jonathan said it came from Santa Claus but I already knew there was no Father Christmas. It was your big brother. Anne gave Jonathan a pen and pencil set in a wooden oak desk stand.

I don't know how my mother managed to feed us. I never thought about it. I cannot recall physical hunger but then I was only five years old and only started thinking or rather rethinking all these things after I started listening to the voice in my head. That is what the voice does. It let you go over and over things present and past the whole time. It tells you what could have happened or what may still happen. How things could have been different if only you had been different. How it will be different if you are different. How things in the shadows, just outside vision and reality, are lurking in your brain ready to pounce on you. That you have to protect yourself all the time. The only thing is it doesn't tell you what to protect yourself from. It destroys time. It is like wave after wave that washes all goodness from the soil just to leave you coarse and sterile and white.

It was the best year of my life. I was five years old, nearly six. I started school two weeks after that Christmas: three days after Jonathan had left for the Army. He was going to be a Gunner in the Artillery. That was five days after the man on the bicycle was killed on the main road just outside the gate into the lane leading up to the farm house and our thatched roof rondavel. The man was killed two days before New Year's Eve. Jonathan left for the Army on the day of the funeral.

Chapter 12

We all went to see what had happened on the main road just across from the turnoff to our house.

I have not yet told you about my other brother and sister but I will do that later, I promise. Maybe when I get to the point where my mom dies or maybe sooner or maybe later. But I will introduce you to them, I promise. They are important to me but I don't want to confuse my story more than what is necessary. I already find it extremely stressful just to keep going in some sort of ever forward time measured motion. I am sorry.

The dead man was lying next to the road. His bicycle, a wreck was dumped next to him. There was no blood. I have seen lots of blood when a sheep is slaughtered or a chicken caught and its head chopped off for Sunday lunch but there was no blood on the body of this man. We were all standing around waiting on the police to arrive.

The sun was starting to set when the police pickup van eventually arrived. There was no blue light flashing. Just two young constables in uniform that jumped out. They were in a hurry. That is what they said. "We are in a hurry."

I could feel Jonathan tightening his grip on my hand when the two constables grabbed the body of the man; one grabbing the hands, the other one the feet and dumped it into the back of the police van. I wanted to put my hands over my ears but Jonathan was holding my right hand too tight. Then the van took off with spinning wheels that kicked the little gravel stones next to the tar road onto us and the broken bicycle of the dead man.

They did not zip the dead man in a body bag. That is what Jonathan said that night when we were all sitting on the big double bed in the rondavel. "They did not even put the body in a body bag." He said that while he was plucking at the fine lose fluff on the blanket. Jonathan always did that when we all were sitting on the double bed, talking at the end of the day or while we were all listening to "The Creaking Door" on the radio if it was a Sunday night. I would then crawl into the bed under the thin blanket between my mom and dad while Jonathan would dim the light to scare us, making sounds like a "*crreeeaaaking*" door with only the light from the moon falling into the room. I wasn't scared.

I thought I knew why they should have put the body in a body bag because the body was all limp like a bag of potatoes. I thought bodies go all limp like cooked spaghetti when one dies. I did not realize that it was because just about every bone in the man's body was broken by the impact of the car. It was a black man from the village on the farm about three hundred meters away from our rondavel. The funeral was on the same day that Jonathan left for his initial nine month military training to become a gunner.

I did not go to the funeral. Nobody went to the funeral but we could hear the people singing at the grave. It was a happy song that wanted me to dance. It wasn't "*In the jungle the mighty jungle*" but it had a similar body swaying beat to it. It was sung without music. I did not know the language. Black people harmonize their voices when they sing. That is what Jonathan said. They had to come and ask the owner of the farm to go and collect the body from the police morgue where it was kept for five days. I think the police should have just left the body at the village, three hundred meters from our rondavel.

The owner of the farm was cross because all the workers on the farm went to the funeral and the grave in the old dusty cemetery plot where they have been burying their ancestors for many years. It was their culture. Everybody must go to appease the spirits. That is what Jonathan said. I should have gone as well. One less spirit may just have swung the balance in my favor.

My dad hated it when Jonathan plucked at the strains of lose wool on the blanket, rolling any that came off into a small dirty ball. My dad said it was thinning the blanket and that he would be cold. Jonathan used to laugh and then pretended to stick the lose fluff back onto the blanket. He would pretend to search for a thin spot on the blanket while he laughed at my dad. We would then all laugh and my dad would just click his tongue.

Chapter 13

Nine months later to the day, we all, the whole family, went to the official military passing out parade after Jonathan completed his military service. He had a small miniature black rifle on his uniform, just above his name to indicate that he was a sniper. He took it off and gave it to Anne his girlfriend, she came with us. My parents liked her. So did I. Jonathan looked at me and said that I will earn my own sharpshooter black rifle one day. I was so proud to walk with him that day. We all were.

Jonathan has taught me to shoot with the pellet gun. Jonathan and I used to shoot the birds in the corn fields on the farm. Jonathan had to score 80% with his army shooting to get the miniature black rifle. I always scored above eighty in all my exams even without studying. That is how I got into Wits University or to give it its full name, The University of the Witwatersrand in Johannesburg, to study engineering. I left university after six months. That was after some of the students burned the old South African flag and the secret police wanted me to join the student movement. Infiltrate is what they called it. I left Wits and joined the Navy.

Anne went to University the same year that Jonathan went to the Army, so she was a year ahead of him when he went to University. But he went to a different university. Jonathan started at Pretoria University while Anne was in her second year at the University of Potchefstroom: Potchefstroom University for Higher Christian Education.

Anne got pregnant by another student the next year, when she was in her third year and never came to visit again.

Jonathan didn't say anything when he came home for the midterm break but I could hear my parents whisper in their bedroom. We were no longer staying on the farm. We had moved into the town and closer to my big school.

Jonathan would get up in the middle of the night to play an old song on the record player in the lounge. It was "*I am the great pretender*" by The Platters. He would play it over and over. He called it a seven single.

The dark of the night never frightened me. It was my own darkness that scared the shit out of me. But maybe I shouldn't say "shit". Maybe I should say "the living daylights!" My mother did not like us to swear. My mother gave me a puppy for my eighth birthday. It was a small black bitch and I named it Lovey. I was tempted to call her Newton because she was close to the ground. Lovey never grew big, she stayed small.

Lovey was sort of the reason why Jonathan's son was born. Lovey died on my thirteenth birthday. That was about a year after Jonathan's son was born. I don't know which was worse.

Chapter 14

I started school when I was six but I have already mentioned that. I hate it when people repeat things but it does give me sense of security. I need routine. That is important. That keeps me calm. It is important for me to stay calm; not to get anxious or paranoid.

I enjoyed school I think, but I am not sure when I think back. I only enjoy it when I don't think about it. I wanted to do tap dancing when I was eight years old. Or maybe it was when I was seven years old. Or was it nine? No, it was when I was eight years old. I think I was eight years old. I only tap danced for two months. I know that. Then I started with karate lessons. I had to buy a uniform. My mother had to buy a uniform. I was a child. I had no money. I went to karate lessons for about two weeks. I shot a hole through my car door when I was about twenty four years old. I think I was twenty four years old but maybe I was twenty five years old or maybe I was twenty three years old. No it was twenty four. I think I was twenty four years old. I will lie in my foetal position tonight when I go to bed and think about it. That, the shooting, was after I burned my forehead with a cigarette, right between my eyes. I carried the scar for the rest of my life. It was a bit like the three circular scars that Buddhist monks get from the three pieces of burning incense that are placed on their heads during their ordination. My single burn did not rid me of bad habits, and above all, it did not rid me of bad thoughts. It also did not give me any wisdom to help release others from suffering.

It was the right front door of my car as you sit behind the steering wheel looking forward though the windscreen. The driver side of the car if it is a right hand drive car as we use in South Africa but we were living in Bophuthatswana at that stage. It would have been the left front door if it was in America. If I had a car and a revolver in America. If I was born in the U.S.A.

That is where I met Dorothy, in Bophuthatswana. She was a Maths teacher and madly in love with me. It is said that mad people do attract certain types of women. Dorothy was a real woman and never used the 'M' word. Not even when I used it to shock people. She left after I kept insisting on us going outside to talk as I didn't want the South African Secret Service to record our personal conversations in my bachelors flat. The flat was in a permanent mess as a result of me looking for the microphones. They were good, the South African Secret Service agents. They cost me Dorothy. I will never forgive them, but maybe I will. They were just doing their job after I made an appointment to see the chief weapons developer at Denel. South African weapons are battle tested and sold to the highest bidder across the world.

They were interested in my idea and I am sure they stole it. Who would not be interested in a rifle bullet that is triggered not by a firing pin, but by a small laser beam that ignites the charge through a prick size glass window? Imagine the speed that can be achieved when not having to wait on a firing pin to be pulled back before it can slam down again. As long as the glass trigger window is tapered like the windows of a submarine but tapered the other way so that the pressure from the ignition of the charge will not blow out the glass window. It need not be glass, it can be crystal. Anything transparent. I don't think submarines have windows. I also had an idea on how to keep the barrel of the rifle cool while firing at this rate.

That is why I went to the science department at Pretoria University with my next idea. They were really interested. The head of the department kept on phoning me at home and we became good friends. I used to use the medical library at Wits University. They, the library staff thought I was a fifth year medical student. I spent a lot of money buying reference books on medicine and phycology and even the odd book on philosophy. Books are more important than food. Books feed the soul.

Chapter 15

I started High School when I was thirteen years old. Actually I turned thirteen after a few days at High School. Thirteen when Lovey was killed by the neighbour's dog.

I pinned a "kick me" note to the back of my Primary School science teacher when I was ten years old. That was after he would not answer my question about evolution. I am sorry, I should not have done that. The school principal phoned my father and he had to attend a meeting at school. The school was not allowed to teach evolution or rather the college that the science teacher attended did not teach evolution. It was the Potchefstroom University for Higher Christian Education.

I am sure I was ten years old.

Murderers on death row also attract certain types of women. It is a mad world.

I am sure the University of Pretoria is still working on my idea of seven outposts in space, hanging in the seven gravity neutral spheres that I have identified for them, slowly rotating their deadly cargo, ready to deposit it with pinpoint accuracy as and when required. I am sure.

It was deeply satisfying working on this idea. It just felt right. I like things to be symmetric: to have just the right balance and harmony. It was simply a case of getting the balance just right. A case of getting the gravitational pull to cancel itself out by using the dominant long range inter-planetary forces. It was simply a matter of getting the counterbalances perfect. It was easy once I knew what I was looking for. It was simply a case of looking at it in a lopsided way. Looking inward into the structure of a hydrogen atom, the simplest atom. That and then to tweak a few charges.

It was an idea that took shape after I read Alice's Adventures in Wonderland. Or rather after I have studied both Alice's Adventures in Wonderland and Through the Looking-Glass. I felt a kinship with the Chester cat – meow! Imagine drinking mirror milk. I am sure that is why Leonardo da Vinci wrote in mirror font.

I left High School two years early. I was bored and did my final two years of formal High School training via a correspondence course in six months. Jonathan once again warned me and my parents that it was foolish and the fact that it worked for my dad does not mean it is the right way for me. Jonathan felt that I required symmetry in my life!

I am sure Pretoria University is still working on my ideas. I am sure. Meow.

Chapter 16

Dorothy and I had long sleepless nights discussing life and the universe and I moved back in with my parents when she just upped and left. We used to sit on a park bench or on a blanket or in the car, talking for hours: the car with a bullet hole in the door. Talking in a safe place where we could not be overheard.

That was after they banned me from the casino. After I got onto the Black Jack table telling them. "You are the reason our social and economic life has changed. You are the reason families have become separated. You and money god Mammon are the reason that consumption culture has taken over."

Mafikeng, the capital of Bophuthatswana had more than one casino; Casinos, the legacy of Apartheid – the destroyer of rural family life in the black homelands. I could sense that something important was being lost, could taste the doom of the destroying plastic pressure of the west descending on these simple people. Could see a future when the beautiful simplicity of their lives have been destroyed. When gaps of culture and outlook will open up between generations. When a self-resourced way of life will be no longer. I was once again a five year old leaving Namibia. It is a burden too much to lose your root intimacy and I am sorry. Sorry that the only asset worth keeping is shrinking to nothing. Sorry that I am losing touch with reality. Sorry that I have fallen through so many worm-holes. Sorry that I have lost Dorothy trying to save the only asset worth protecting.

We, Dorothy and I used to spend a lot of time at the casinos. Not always to gamble but it had air-conditioning and comfortable chairs with noise that would make it just about impossible to record any conversation and little drinks with colourful umbrellas. My dad liked to gamble. He could play poker on the poker slot machines for hours. He ever only told us about the wins. Never about the losses. My dad was working as a chemist in Mafikeng.

Someone, I wouldn't like to mention names, remarked years later that she had bumped into Dorothy in Durban and that Dorothy begged her not to tell me where she was or even that she had bumped into her. Dorothy said that she was afraid of me.

I don't understand that. I have never hurt anybody in my life.

I even wrote her, Dorothy, a number of stories and poems during my clear moments or may it be just the other way round. Can it be that I can only put my thoughts onto paper when I am not clear of mind? Are those closest to me in danger when I am not clear of mind? I am so sorry. My hurt is more than any hurt that I can possibly inflict. I am so sorry.

I would have liked it to travel. To get onto a plane or boat and visit new places but I was afraid. Afraid of what may happen in a strange place if I go mental. Afraid that I may end up in a jail where they will throw the keys away. My fear, plus my medical history of mental issues would have prevented me from getting into another country even if I wanted to. Even if I could get myself to go. And this before the visit of the police after I went away to Durban for a weekend at the beach with friends.

I would really have liked it to go to Ireland where it is never dry. Where there is rain every day and the grass is green all year round. Ireland where there are no dry riverbeds, no enclosed concrete reservoirs and no desert. That was before I found out about the Magdalene laundries!

I have cut and pasted one of my love stories to Dorothy at the end of this. I have even changed the font so as to not confuse my story to Dorothy with my reality. So please have a read when you get to the end.

Chapter 17

My Very Educated Mother Just Showed Us Nine Planets. How stupid is that! Not that my mom is stupid but everybody should just know the names of our planets: Mercury, Venus, Earth, Mars, Jupiter, Saturn, Uranus, Neptune, Pluto and planet X.

It is like knowing the Times Tables. Everybody should just know all the tables from 1 X 1 = 1 to 12 X 12 = 144 by heart. It is like instinctively feeling your left side. Left is where your heart beats stronger. Not that the heart is really on the left. It just gives the sense that it is on the left. There are certain universal truths. There are laws that govern the universe and that control us. We are part of the universe. A universe where electrons revolve around the nucleus of an atom; where planets revolve around the sun. And that is what controls my schizophrenic universe: those rogue electrons and the rogue planets. Those things that don't conform. Those things that I can't foresee. Those things that I have to think about all the time to keep myself in sync. To keep myself in balance. To keep my atoms together with their internal attraction of opposite charges. Have to keep the numbers adding up. Have to keep the mathematical universe in which all things exist in sync. Have to live with and within the splitting of my own mental functions.

I know I have what may be perceived as a problem. I know that sometimes but what if I am right? I must be right. I know I am right. What if there is something somewhere emitting photons? What if antimatter is slowly annihilating the universe? So why is that called paranoia?

The electrons on the outer circle wobble. They don't follow a defined circle. Worse, they sometimes leave their circle and join the electrons from a neighbouring atom. They distort the universe. Your electrons, or some of your electrons may end up in my body, in my universe and some of my electrons may AWOL into your domain. We are shared. We all become a pot of jelly wobbling through space and time.

I sometimes move outwards. I move away from this simple nine planet solar system, away from this galaxy and this universe and cosmos and look down on all the atoms, each with its own nucleus of protons and circling electrons, and try and see Earth. Try and see whether I am an atom in the toe or nose or bladder of the body of the universe.

I sometimes fall inwards. Into the nucleus of my atom. Drill down past quarks and electrons, past neutrinos, Higgs Bosons and photons, into a new universe within a universe within until I run out of air. Until being a universe becomes too much. Until it all becomes too much and then I have to recite Psalm 23. Then I have to go back to the beginning to tougher myself again anew or if I am lucky, to relive the good again, but that is not often. That will not be right. Or rather it is right but it stresses me out! It is difficult to relive the good in vivid 3-D Technicolor while dark clouds of paranoia scream to be heard. It is difficult to live in more than one world at the same time.

Chapter 18

I was twelve years old and my sister was still living at home. We, the four of us: my sister and I and our parents went on holiday. We did not go away on holiday often. I guess my dad was too restless by nature or felt strangely trapped when he had to have a good time. A good time to him was doing his own thing even if it meant balancing sheets of numbers, rows and rows of columns like petrol pump readings when the forecourt shifts changed or reconciling bank statements.

My dad could add and subtract any number of amounts of any value without ever carrying ones to tens to hundreds to thousands to ten thousands to eternity. My dad could just not sit still until after he lost his vocal cords and most of his hearing. After he was found slumped over the desk at the garage that he managed for my brother. The brother that I haven't told you about yet. Then my dad had no problem to sit in front of the TV going at full blast. Those were my good old days. The days after my dad had a stroke without any of us realising it and he started doing his shuffle walk; a bit like a duck doing the quick-step. I also worked at my brother's garage but that only came much later. Now I was twelve and we were going on holiday.

We took a family trip to the Victoria Falls. I always found it questionably interesting that The Falls were discovered by someone being carried through the African jungle on a chair. Carried there by the descendants of the locals that have lived for generations at the foot of the Smoke that Thunders.

The world's largest sheet of falling water is impressive even when you are twelve years old and even when seeing it with your parents and sister. Even more so when your disease is still in its infancy. It is always later, in retrospect that a life already lived becomes a problem.

We stayed at a beautiful old colonial hotel and were greeted by the staff in crisp white Victorian uniforms like long lost explorers every time that we entered or left the shade of the old thatched patios where they served large jugs of Pimms to the adults. My mother loved it. They, my parents even looked like a couple in love. They just didn't love me. Or maybe they did but that was before Jonathan's son was born. Before their prayers returned empty and they were burdened by two broken children: a son and a grandson, both with the same names. It is true: the sins of the fathers shall be visited upon their children.

It is difficult to enjoy anything if you question everything. More so if you have to question everything. Impossible when you have to question yourself all the time. My dad changed jobs very frequently. We moved a lot. We stayed in many different houses in different towns across different counties. My poor mother. My dad seldom lasted in a job even for as long as I had survived in the Navy and then the physiatrist had the audacity to suggest that my mental short wiring may be coming from her side of the family.

I had no children. My sin is my own cross to bear. It is totally above any understanding how a cross could have become the sign of salvation. The spiritual world is madder than me.

And I don't understand the First World's obsession with throwing money at things when it is broken. Or their obsession with prolonging life at all cost. It is so sad, so wasteful. It is so degrading to put a paper value on everything. To plaster things over with paper and then to walk away washing all sin of your hands. It is playing god from a distance.

Chapter 19

Jonathan's son James Clark was born weighing barely two pound. He was born ten weeks prematurely two days before my dad's birthday, but baby James only went home the day before Christmas when he weighed five pounds. He was nearly two months old when he finally went home to Jonathan and his wife.

Baby James came to stay with us when he was five years old. He stayed with us for a year before he went into a fulltime care home. My mother, and I think my father loved Baby James more than they ever loved me. Baby James required care 24 hours a day every day, seven days a week. There was no time left in the day for me. Not even after Jonathan got a black woman to help with Baby James. Jonathan warned my mom and dad but they did not want to listen. It took them a year to admit that he was right once again. A year before they agreed that Baby James needed more than what they could provide. My father changed after that. He became all withdrawn and started drinking more.

When I was five and shortly after we moved from Windhoek, we stayed on a farm. There were pigs on the farm and I wanted to hold one of the piglets that were running around making funny noises. The piglets were putting their pink noses into the dirt and had little curly tails and never stopped talking in their high pitched squalling pig language.

I often thought how Baby James's disability limited his world. That his world was limited to the now: his bed, his room and most importantly to his next meal. The maid would push him in his special buggy to go and get milk and bread from the shop around the corner, barely a 100 metres away. That was the size of Baby James's whole world. Baby James's world was too small. My worlds were too big. My worlds were bigger than the universe or the cosmos.

I often wished I had his too small world. I know he wanted my world, my too big worlds. I also know that he loved Jonathan more than even I did. Jonathan was his hero and mine. Jonathan used to say that he would have wished to be a Zulu if he was a black South African. A Zulu warrior, an induna that can sit in front of his hut while the wives brought him beer and his children played in front of him in the veld. Baby James would have liked that world. There would have been a whole village of people willing to look after him.

The piglets' world was the dump on the farm and Jonathan was leopard crawling towards them. Jonathan was on a weekend pass from the Army. I could see the sow, the mother of the pink piglets, storming towards Jonathan flat on his stomach. The sow was on his back as he reached out to lift the closest screaming wiggling pink piglet. Jonathan dropped the piglet and turned around. All in one swift movement and jammed his right fist and most of his arm down the sow's throat. The squealing piglet ran away and the mother chased after it. It was a blessing that Jonathan was fit from his military training.

I don't eat pork. Not even bacon. I have never ever touched a pig. Pigs don't exist in any of my worlds. Pigs only exist in my nightmares when I am in Baby James's world. Where I can't move or talk. Where my tongue is swollen. Where I am totally dependent on someone else's love 24 hours a day, and when that becomes too much for them and they run out of love.

Chapter 20

I got Lovey for my eighth birthday. I must have got other presents as well but I can't remember it. I normally don't forget anything but I can't remember my eight birthday except that Lovey was there and I had a purpose.

Maybe I can't recall anything from my eight birthday because I had very little sleep the first few nights after my eight birthday. I did not want to leave Lovey alone for a second and she needed my attention all the time. She was a three week old puppy that my mom found in a bag next to the main road. She was with her two brothers or maybe it was two sisters or maybe a brother and sister. The others puppies were dead.

I picked her name: Lovey.

There was a knock on our door and Jonathan answered. There was a young lady standing and her car had broken down just outside our house. We were staying in a different house once again and Jonathan was working at the magistrate's offices. Jonathan told the young woman to have a seat while he looked at her car. It only took him a few minutes to fix it and she was really pleased.

"Come Lovey" Jonathan said when she got up to go back to her car. Jonathan was talking to my Lovey, the dog but this young lady did not know that. She blushed and gave Jonathan her phone number. They got married eighteen months later.

I will never forget my thirteenth birthday. We were staying in a house with a swimming pool and we were having a BBQ, except that it is called a Braai in South Africa. The gates to the property were open so that our neighbours could join us. Their dog followed them and chased Lovey onto the patio where he ripped her stomach open. She died in my arms.

Jonathan was away doing a three month camp in the army. He was away in the army preparing for a war that could never be won.

It was then, after Lovey was killed, that my parents first realised that there was something wrong with me: something serious.

Chapter 21

My dad could not accept that there was something wrong with Jonathan's son, Baby James. Baby James, my dad's first, and as it would later be proven, his only grandson. My dad could play any musical instrument. My dad also believed that Baby James would one day pick up his mattress and walk. So did Baby James. He believed it too. Grandfather and grandson both lived in the time of yesterday, stuck in one of their universes, until grandfather couldn't anymore. Then Baby James went into a care home to wait at the gate on his mattress.

In reality, Baby James should not have survived. It was a miracle that Baby James pulled through.

I was in the car with Jonathan when he had to go to the hospital for the birth. There was no time to take me home first.

Baby James was born shortly after Jonathan got to the hospital. He weighed barely two old-world pounds, not even a kilogram and showed only signs of life at birth. However, Baby James's will to live was stronger than mine. His will to live was stronger than the will of any of us to live. That was clear from that moment the sister told Jonathan that she would not again tap, with her forefinger, against Baby James's little wild pigeon breast to get his heart going again. This was while we were waiting outside the ICU, peeping through the glass wall. It was there where Baby James was lying naked in the warm incubator in the intensive care unit of the clinic. That was after the sisters inside the brightly lit glass room had thrown open the door because they had thought Jonathan had passed out where he and I had been standing outside, alone, hour after hour. Pain shared is not always pain halved.

Baby James was the first grandchild on both sides. Baby James is the first grandchild with the Clark surname. Baby James never did anybody any harm. Baby James's survival was the biggest single tragedy and sorrow in many lives, not only in mine. The price for Baby James's survival was higher and longer than all the other tragedies and sorrows of both the two families thrown together. It was my biggest tragedy. It was my shipwreck.

Baby James did not grow up but he did develop an interest in soccer, soccer and South African country music on television. Baby James cannot speak. Cannot feed himself. Can barely swallow and definitely not clap hands. He also cannot use his legs, but he can follow soccer on television and has his own team that he supports blindly and loyally. Baby James understands Afrikaans and English and more than one black African language, including Zulu. He also laughs with Jonathan when his younger sisters begin with stories like the "Three Little Pigs". My nephew, Baby James has never caused anybody any harm and has my father's clear blue eyes. Just like me.

Maybe it is sometimes better to look away. To not stand outside an ICU looking in from the outside. Better to be the god in the distance. Not to get involved. Maybe it is better to live the dream. The sun rises and the sun sets. To die is to stop dying. True words, but not mine: the words of the Afrikaans poet with the green jersey, Breyten Breytenbach.

My dad finally gave up. He could not live in that universe any longer. Not after the day when he carried Baby James into the bank and afterwards said that the people didn't know how to respond to Baby James and him. That they made place for them so he could just walk directly up to the counter with the heavy nearly six-year-old ragdoll-child in his arms. And that just before eleven on a busy month-end Saturday morning...

My dad should have carried me when I needed him and now it was too late. Lovey is dead.

Chapter 22

I started my compulsory military service for a white God and Country in June. The year does not matter. I had no choice. All white South African males had to go to the army. I was lucky. I was trained down to Cape Town by the military with thousands of other bewildered white young men. I was just one amongst many. My voice went with me. My mother was pleased in a concerned way. Mothers know. The voice hated that.

My parents gave up on my disease but not on me. I could not blame them. They made it my brother's problem. Jonathan is a bit more than ten years older than me. I used to take his socks from the dirty washing basket to smell when he went away to boarding school in Windhoek. I was three years old. He could only come home one weekend in six. There was no high school in our town. It was only later when my parents moved to Windhoek that he could be a day scholar again. That only lasted until we had to move to Johannesburg. Then Jonathan had to go back to boarding school. Nothing good ever lasts.

I started writing letters to the commanding officer and the medical officer while in the Navy. That was a mistake and I realised it. I then wrote letters to recall the first letters. It was an even bigger mistake. It got out of my hands.

I was discharged from the South African Defence Force for medical reasons after six months. Actually I was in the Navy but it is the same family. It was never my family. I should never had gone but it was not my choice. The universe it her wisdom decides all things.

I took all the money from my dad's wallet, tore it up and flushed it down the toilet. My guilt kicked in so I broke the window to stage a robbery but I did it in such a way that it was obvious that it was not a real robbery. I broke the bedroom window from the inside. I did not want an innocent person, even an unknown one, to be blamed for my actions. I had to do it. I had to flush the money down the toilet. There are more important things than money. The voice is always right. Thank god I only had one voice. It did not make the pain of my guilt easier but we all have to share the burden; just not in equal measures. We have to empty the cup given to us. Even if we have to write from right to left as reading it in a mirror. Each one in his or her own mirror while distancing oneself, looking in from a distance. Just ask Leonardo Da Vinci. He had no father either. His mother was also sold off. The difference is that she didn't want him either and he had no big brother.

I was born lucky.

Chapter 23

The Army medics had to come and get me down from the signal tower at Saldana Naval Base just outside Cape Town when I couldn't get down. When I could not let go of the steel tower. Not even after the first injection to relax my muscles frozen in the hot summer evening.

My brother was my first and only non-military visitor.

Jonathan flew up from Johannesburg to Cape Town to drive my car home. I was not allowed to drive. I only learned later how to beat the system. That was once I realised that they were watching me 24 hours a day every day. That the lights behind the Flat Mountains belonged to an alien vessel. That they knew that as well but that they did not want me to know. That the voice told me that I am right even when I doubted it and that was often. The same voice that told me to put my bed on seven feet stilts so that I slept with my face just shy of the ceiling. The same voice that told me to sleep on just a blanket on the floor. The same voice that told me to wash my hands ten times in an hour. The same voice that told me to not to bath or wash or brush my teeth for weeks on end. The same voice that told me at thirty one to tie the tie around my neck while sitting under the tree in the peaceful garden on a Sunday afternoon after church.

The same voice that told me that they had a cosmic vacuum sucking up all the rogue electrons. That they are building a parallel universe. That I will never be able to stay ahead.

Chapter 24

Psychiatric hospitals and wards aren't so bad. I know, I was in quite a few for different lengths of time: from a single day to months on end and often on a voluntary basis, I think. Or did they make me think that?

It was boring, but it was routine. I would have hated it to be mental in the olden days when mental institutions had to put on shows to collect money. When they poured cold water over the inmates so that the audience could have a good old fall down laugh. Or just imagine getting electric shock therapy as in "One Flew Over the Cuckoo's Nest"!

"Vintery, mintery, cutery, corn,
Apple seed and apple thorn,
Wire, briar, limber lock,
Three geese in a flock.
One flew east,
And one flew west,
And one flew over the cuckoo's nest!"

Anyway being away in an institution gave my parents a break. They never visited. My father never liked the smell of hospitals. Mental hospitals and psychiatric wards don't smell like hospitals. Not really.

The school bully once punched me so hard that I had to get stiches on the inside of my mouth. We were standing in our queues waiting to enter our classroom when I intervened. He, Lucas the school bully was picking on another much smaller boy. That time my dad had no choice. He had to take me to the hospital.

They taught us coping skills in some of the institutions. Only in some of them. Or rather they tried to teach us things liking breathing exercises for when you can feel a panic attack coming on or when your anxiety becomes too much. I preferred to chant. To chant silently in my head. To recite Psalm 23 over and over and over again silently in my head. To think of every word, every verse. To visualise the shepherd walking into the river so that the scared sheep can drink over his shoulder, the still waters dammed in his circled arms. To visualise him walking in front leading the way through the Valley of Death. Waiting for him to lift my burden and let me lie down.

It was interesting to meet the new staff, especially the young ones doing their internships. Fresh out of University and shocked by the behaviour of some of us inmates. Some of us did it on purpose but in a nice way. Never to hurt.

I can recall the pretty one. I just knew she didn't wear panties. It is just one of those things that one knows. We were sitting in our huddle group, sharing thoughts but only if you wanted to. Never any pressure but your own. Wanting to be part while being absent. To delve and to shock. To leave your own body and look down on the group. She looked at me. It was my turn.

"She comes to me in the middle of the night. She is so pretty that a single drop of her spit will turn all the water in the oceans into fresh water."

She refolded her legs, right over left, confirming what I had already known.

"I now sleep with a cross between my legs."

They all believed me! I was pulling a fast one and they believed me.

I had a massive wet dream that night even though one of the many side effects of my medication was a suppression of libido.

I wish she would not call me Jim. I wish she would use my real name James, James Clark.

Chapter 25

I had a teenage party once and I also invited Lucas the bully. Lucas that hit me so hard that I had to have stiches in my jaw on the inside of my mouth. I could not eat properly for days. I thought it was a good idea to invite him as well. My mother used to say: "Turn the other cheek" when you complained that someone did you wrong. That must be the worse advice ever but I only realised it after the party or rather during the party when Lucas broke into my dad's drinks cabinet.

My mother also used to say: "Sit at the back so that you can be moved to the front." That never happened. All that ever happened was that the teachers thought you were up to no good.

Both my brothers warned my mother that they should stay at home when I have a party. They warned her that is was not Windhoek but Johannesburg. My mother knew better or maybe it was because I said I am not a baby and she should trust me. It was a mistake. It took me the whole night and the rest of the day to clean the house.

There was dried egg yolk against the walls in the passage and tomato sauce on the carpets. Everything in the fridge was dumped on the kitchen floor. I never had another party ever again. I stayed clear of Lucas at school. Being mental does not mean being stupid. Only democratically elected governments make the same old mistakes over and over again, invading lessor countries to destabilise the world in the name of freedom for the masses. Masses that are incapable to drive a car never mind run a country.

I did have a special birthday party when I turned seven. It was under the tree in the garden and my mom used her special tall wine glasses. The glasses gave a tint of all the colours of the rainbow when the sun played on it. Jonathan went to the planetarium in Johannesburg close to the University of the Witwatersrand and got me a set of glass light spectrum lenses. This opened up a new world to me. I am still intrigued by the way that a glass prism can split light into different groups of colour. Light is like my world; made up of many different worlds that you don't know about until you know about it.

I had such a terrible headache on my special seventh birthday party that I can recall my headache better than the actual party but Jonathan's present was the best. Newton is my only other hero. Isaac Newton the son of an illiterate father that died before he, Isaac Newton, was born. And then a stepfather that hated the sight of him. A stepfather that was a reverend. That was *Isaacus Neutonus* "God's Holy One". A man after my own image.

Chapter 26

I tried. I really tried time and time again.

I got a job. I started an IBM mainframe computer COBOL programming course. I met a pretty blonde girl. I got married. I went mad and when I got home she was gone. Johanna just upped and left. Love cannot conquer madness. My disease had a smell of its own but not everyone can smell it. Only those sensitive to others. Those that can hear electricity crackling in appliances in the quiet of the night, can smell my disease. And my smell makes them sick. It drives them away. If only I had no smell. If only I was a nothing. But I am a nothing. I ended up wandering the streets with just my thoughts and the voice as company. All of this because of a broken geyser.

Johanna gave me a freshwater aquarium as a wedding present. We were young, stupid and in love. The tank and the two tropical blue discus fish were waiting when we got back from our one night honeymoon. She had organised with the owner of the specialist pet shop to have it set-up while we were away.

Then the geyser broke down. It wasn't leaking but it was not heating the water either. I was the man of the house and called out a plumber a few days later. My dad said not to worry. The body corporate looking after our complex will sort out the bill.

I should have known better. I was now a married man, I got married even after Jonathan had a serious talk with both Johanna and me. Smoke and mirrors are only good for magic tricks. My mom had an emergency triple bypass and the medical bills were never paid. The same as the bills for the school or the butcher or the lawyer or Jonathan's different boarding schools all those many years ago.

"Rich Man,
Poor Man,
Beggar Man,
Thief!"

Jonathan gave us his blessings after the wedding. He took us away to the honeymoon hotel. We were sitting at the back holding hands and he was driving, talking to us while looking in the rear-view mirror.

The bailiff came calling and I was again five years old opening the door at our house in Windhoek. The man wanted to see my mother. He did not say a word to her, just asked her for her left hand and removed her engagement ring. My mom said nothing. Only later, many years later did I hear it was the bailiff from the bankruptcy court. That my grandmother had told people about my mother's big clear blue diamond engagement ring. It took me weeks in an institution before I could go home again.

The two blue discus freshwater fish were still there. I have no idea who looked after them as they required lots of attention. But they did not look healthy. They looked lifeless and the one was floating on top of the water two days later. I flushed it down the toilet and sat next to the tank for three days solid, looking at the other one. Eventually I had to take a rest. I took a sterile needle and stabbed the discus between the eyes trying to kill it in a humane way. I then flushed it down the toilet. I went outside a few minutes later to open the manhole cover looking for it. I wanted to make sure it was dead. I did not want it to suffer.

I moved back in with my parents.

I heard years later that Johanna had a daughter. A pretty girl with curly blond hair and bright smiley soul blue eyes. A single mother bringing up a pretty little girl barely ten miles from where I was staying.

Chapter 27

My dad was mugged on the way to The Bank and I did not believe him. I have lived with poverty my whole life. My dad was on his way to deposit the days' takings from the garage where both of us worked. It was not my brother's garage. That only came later.

It was violent times prior to the run-up of the first free-and-fair elections in South Africa. "Free and fair". The world had no idea. There was an undercurrent of pending doom, but in an exciting way. Like static electricity in the air and I was asked to leave the home and go home. Go back to my parents. The government in their last days and months in power were concerned that all medical facilities may come under strain if the political lid should blow off. I was not alone, everybody was paranoid. It was exciting times. I started doing odd jobs at the garage that my dad managed.

I had, on a previous occasion and before the mugging, found my dad's empty wallet in the walkway next to the house. I opened it, saw that it was empty and dropped it again. I watched it for days until it just one day disappeared. Watching it was one of my obsessions and it trapped me for days. I was relieved when it finally disappeared but then I started obsessing as to where it had disappeared to. Of who or what took it. I realised that I had to increase my medication or go back into an institute. There were none available. I kept on thinking about the broken bicycle that also just disappeared from next to the road all those years ago when I was five years old. The one day there the next day gone.

The money to be deposited was in a canvas bank bag with the deposit book already completed, hidden under the seat of the car seat on which my dad was sitting, when he stopped at the four way stop. South Africa uses four way stops rather than roundabouts. My dad was second in line at the stop, waiting his turn when the car door was opened and someone jumped in, pistol in hand. According to my dad it happened so quickly that he had no time to react. The bag with money was snapped from under him before he could even blink. He had no time to reach for his revolver that he carried strapped around his ankle.

It did not make sense to me. How did this person know where the bag was? Why didn't my dad just lift his foot from the clutch and attacked the guy or bumped into the car in front of him? Why did he not jump out of the car and chased after the mugger? Why did he not just shoot the low lying bastard? That would have proven my dad's innocence to me. It would have made him a hero and not only to me.

Where do things go when they disappear? I understand that there are mite that feed on dead skin and barely visible creatures that thrive on the snot-balls that people drop when they pick their noses, but what about bigger things like paperclips or socks or shopping trollies?

Chapter 28

It was just after six o'clock in the morning when the alarm went off. The alarm was linked to the garage and motor dealer where my dad was working. I first thought that my dad may have triggered it when he opened the main office but a little voice, a different voice told me different. I was on my medication. It may even be that I felt guilty about my dad's missing wallet. But I knew something was seriously wrong and it was not my voice talking.

I was on the garage forecourt well before Jonathan but not before the ambulance. I could not control myself. I did not need the voice. I just went berserk. I have had this un-controlling fear ever since I turned twelve that my dad will die before I am an adult. That he will leave me. I was twelve when Jonathan had his son. I went mental and started shouting at the petrol jockeys on the forecourt. It was their fault. It was an inside job. I threw stones at them, anything that I could lay my hands on. I arrived at the hospital long after Jonathan even though he had a shower first after my mom phoned him. I could not blame him. My dad had cried "wolf" too often.

My dad was laying in his own blood. The smell of blood was everywhere. It looked as if he was floating on top of his own blood even though he wasn't bleeding anymore. He was talking, reassuring me that he was fine but that he needed to go to the toilet. That was not possible. He was going into surgery. He had a stab wound just below his eye but not into his brain. His glasses saved his life. He had another stab wound through his hand and into his chest. His hand saved his life. The knife stopped just short of his heart. He was forced to open the safe in the office with a bleeding hand while the people were having their cars filled with fuel just meters away. My dad was relieved of the revolver that he carried strapped around his ankle, as he went down after the first stab to his eye. Someone that knew was waiting behind the door as he opened it going into the admin office. There was nothing on the CCTV tape. It was an inside job.

My dad could not go to the toilet, before he was wheeled into the operating theatre, but the nurse did bring him a bedpan and left it to Jonathan while she waited outside the little curtained cubicle. It sounded as if Thor had struck the white canvas stretcher with his hammer. Even the nurse was giggling when Jonathan handed her the empty bedpan. I knew then that my dad was going to be fine. It was one of the few things that I knew for certain.

My dad recovered. He always did and he went back to work at the garage. I can't say the same of myself. I did not go back to work at that garage ever again. Not even to visit or to have my car filled.

I started selling sweets outside the entrance to our local train station.

Chapter 29

Isaac Newton had to go back and farm after his stepfather, the Reverend Barnabas Smith died. He had to go back and farm. He was seventeen. I have no idea how long he kept it up. I do know that he was not a farmer. His mom also realised it and sent him back to school. That was his turning point. He graduated with top marks and went to Trinity College, Cambridge of course.

I started selling sweets until my paranoia kicked in with vengeance so I shaved my beard and stayed at home, sleeping during the day and wandering at night. I forgot to eat and when I did it was standing up. I lost total track of what is called reality and I knew it. That was the worst part: knowing it and not being able to stop it.

I shaved my beard because Jonathan mentioned that I must have become conservative. He said I looked like an AWB member; a member of the Afrikaner resistance movement. I knew the secret police was once again onto me. I knew that they had never left me.

I was selling cheap sweets just outside the barbed wire fence to the station. I had to ask my mom for the money: an advance for my latest venture. I once again disappointed her. I never paid her back. My sister in Australia transferred money into my mom's bank account the day after my mom passed away. By then it was too late. I had no turning point in my life and I am sorry, so sorry.

I was frightened by the competition at the station. Others saw me selling sweets from my portable plastic table and followed my example. They added cigarettes and matches. They started selling single cigarettes. I could not compete.

I ate the remainder of my sweets over the next few days but never grew my beard again. Not even after I started work at my quiet brother's 24-hour garage cum convenience store, but that came only much later. Enough to say that we had fuel in our veins. We were always involved in or with garages. Even after my dad went bankrupt running his own two garages in Windhoek. The garages were called Alpha and Beta. Isn't that ironic? There was never a "Gamma".

Chapter 30

My dad was caught up in a bank robbery and nearly shot by accident. The random bullet fired by a nervous bank robber passed through the wooden leg of the chair in which the security guard was sitting when the bank was robbed. My dad was queuing to deposit the money from the garage. It was one of my dad's longer-term jobs. He must have felt guilty about the violence that had followed him since he started at that garage.

I was intrigued by the bullet hole in the chair. I should say that I was mesmerised by it and I went back to ask to look at it numerous times until the bank manager contacted my dad to tell me to stop visiting the bank, asking to see the chair. The chair was no longer there. It was taken away to be destroyed as it was no longer safe to be used as a chair. I did not see it as a chair just to be sit on. It had become the engineer's chair to me: the missing link in a cosmic puzzle. They should have given the chair to me. The garage was a VIP customer!

The bullet left a perfect round hole in the wooden leg. Where did the content of the hole go? I can understand some molecules were compressed sideways, fused into the neighbouring wood. Some particles were blown out but what about the rest of the invisible wooden splinters dispersed into the air? Where did that go? I should have paid more attention to my dad's stab wounds. I should have insisted that it was not stitched up until I had a proper look. How do things hang together when the internal balance is distorted? How did I keep on functioning?

The chair, any chair is only visible because we see it as a chair. We don't see the 99% of it that is invisible. We don't see the universe upon universe of emptiness between the atoms. Did the bullet pass through my dad without touching any of his atoms? Did every atom in the bullet, traveling at 900 feet per second and every atom in my dad's physical body in rest, line up perfect just this once?

It was just after three o'clock in the morning when I knocked on Jonathan's window. I had dropped a Coca Cola bottle when I got home and it had exploded. A piece of the glass from the exploding Coke bottle under pressure managed to open up quite a wound in my leg and I realised that I needed medical attention or bleed to death. I should not have bothered but the majority rule of the "yes" molecules in my body won, and I ended up at A & E.

The shock of the accident, with the exploding glass bottle, has worn off by this stage, and I could have a proper look at the actual wound. It was really interesting. The cut was cleaned and most of the blood flow was stopped and I was waiting on the surgeon, so time was on my side. There were white little fat cells bubbling out of the wound and I could speed-up the boiling pot by squeezing the wound just ever so slightly. I had to stop when I realised that Jonathan was going to faint.

Chapter 31

My dad was diagnosed with throat cancer and had his vocal cords removed.

He came home.

I went to my bedroom, closed the door and cried. I cried and cried. I cried for my dad and I cried for me. I cried for the five year old me that I had left behind. I cried for my children that I knew would never be born. I cried for my nephew Jonathan. I cried for the world. I did not know that my dad would outlive me. That my dad would one day get into his car every Saturday morning, like clockwork, to drive to Jonathan and that the two of them would then go for breakfast; father without a voice and his oldest son. I did not know then that my voiceless father would get into his car most Sundays, to drive to the middle of nowhere to attend church with me. A church in hell.

All that I knew was that I was lost.

My dad was a forty a day man. He was a heavy smoker and I should have known. He should have known. Both my parents smoked. My mom smoked because my dad taught her to smoke. She said she didn't want to kiss him before she started smoking. She died for love. She also had four children.

Jonathan said that he used to pretend he was sleeping when he was a baby. He said he would keep his eyes shut and hold his breath when my mom used to bent over his Moses Basket. Just not to smell the smoke on her breath. Jonathan said there was nothing that he could do about the cigarette ash that ended up in the basket with him. Jonathan hated smoking.

My dad did not die from cancer. My mom died from a massive cardiac arrest when everybody was gravely concerned about my dad. I did not think my mom would die, even after she was admitted to hospital on that Sunday morning. She phoned Jonathan and his wife organised for the ambulance to take her to our local hospital.

My dad still wanted to smoke even after his voice box was removed and he had to breathe through a hole in his throat. A hole that he kept covered with cravats made by my other brother's wife. My dad should have studied Sigmund Freud's life. Freud had numerous operations for mouth cancer but even then, he still insisted on smoking by levering his mouth open with a clothes pin. "Men will always be mad, and those who think they can cure them are the maddest of all" a la Voltaire. I wonder whether I would have died if I had worn a cravat instead of a tie.

My dad and I went to see my mom after she was admitted and then went back to work. I had to stand-in for my mom. Managing my brother's 24 hours-a-day garage requires just that; 24 hours a day commitment. I should have known better. I should have heard what the medical staff was trying to tell us.

The hospital phoned three hours later, just as the shifts were changing at the garage. My dad never finished that day's fuel pump readings but he was back that evening. He had to keep busy while I went mad once again. I lost my ability to cry.

Chapter 32

I have seen dead bodies before but this was different. This was my mother.

I was looking down on the raised bed as if from a distance. I was present in the hospital room but removed. I could sense the nurse trying to usher us from the room; sympathetic but professional. She had a job to do.

I was looking down at a body distorted by a massive heart attack, hands like claws trying to fend off death, teeth drawn back in horror and I was thinking of what Jonathan had said when I once asked him what it is like to kill someone; the terrorists coming over the Angolan border into neighbouring Namibia where I was born thirty years ago.

Jonathan did not reply for a long time. I wasn't going to ask again. I should not have asked. I knew damn well that he didn't want to think about it, never mind talk about it. Why are we so intrigued by death? Why are we so envious of the young white soldiers that have seen and experienced death? Those that have caused death. They called it "hitting contact". We outside the military used that term as well, "hitting contact" feeling like comrades as if we were part of it.

"My brother has "hit contact"" and everybody would stop what they were doing. You would be the centre of attention, everybody waiting not even breathing. It was not necessary to say more and the different conversations would slowly pick up again. Everybody knew that you were not allowed to say more but for a few seconds or minutes you would be the hero and the men just back from their compulsory military tour or those still to go, would come to you during the rest of the evening or Saturday afternoon next to the BBQ fire and look at you or just bring you a beer. I hated to be the centre of any attention.

"You just distance yourself," Jonathan said. He wasn't looking at me. He was looking into space, not focusing on anything.

"You just say to yourself it wasn't me. I must have missed them even when you knew you could not have. It must have been one or all of the others now helping to clear up. To drag the broken bodies together to be stripped and taken back to camp."

I never asked again and he never mentioned it again. I could however understand that bodies had to be carted off quickly. "Transported off" as they would have said. Namibia is a hot dry country and the sealable body bags were not for terrorists.

The nurse did a really professional job. My mother looked strangely at peace with her mouth and eyes closed. Only her face was not covered by the single white sheet. I lifted the one corner and realised she was completely naked under it. It was not necessary to stay any longer. I had my own fill of hospitals and could, for the first time, understand my father's excuse of the smell of hospitals. It was not the smell of hospitals. It was the smell of death.

My dad did not stay at our apartment that evening. He moved in with my other brother and his wife where they have prepared his own his self-contained room and en-suite bathroom with three meals a day.

It is time to tell you about my other brother and sister as I have promised. Both are younger than Jonathan but older than me as I have mention before. The family fell apart after my mom passed away. That sounds so dramatic: "The family fell apart."

I fell apart.

Chapter 33

My brother Joseph is the quiet one. Much more emotionally stable than the rest of us children. Either that or he can hide it better or because he is the second child. That is what my third, or was it the forth, psychologist said: "Later borns score higher on agreeableness."

Joseph kept very much to himself but was still intense in himself. We are all just numbers. We have no control but to protect ourselves. And sometimes one another.

Joseph and his wife bought a 24 hours-a-day garage. They bought it so that my parents and even I, for a short while, could have a purpose. We worked at the garage. I worked night shift in the 24-hour convenience store. It allowed me to climb onto the roof at night when it was quiet and the whole world sleeping. It reminded me of the plantation workers in The Cider House Rules by John Irving except that I did not sit and drink on the roof.

"They sit on the roof all nights, some nights."
"They get drunk up there and fall off, some nights."
"They break bottles up there and cut themselves up."
"Anyway, nobody pays attention to them rules."

I should have listened to Joseph and stayed off the roof.

It was from on top a roof that I first saw the lights behind the Flat Mountains. My voice went mad.

Joseph used to tickle me at the critical stage during the "Creaking Door" Sunday evening radio show when I was five years old. Just as everybody was holding their breaths with the moonlight throwing moving shadows into the dark room. Jonathan would then turn the light back on and we will miss the final part of the story. My dad would click his tongue. My dad did a lot of tongue clicking on Sundays and my mom would say: "Stop before he wets the bed." I never wet the bed.

Joseph and I used to wrestle on the bed or on the lose rug on the floor and I would win even though I was eight years younger than him. I would end up sitting on top of Joseph and would call to Jonathan: "Look at me, I have won again."

My dad managed Joseph and his wife's garage. Taking the pump readings when the shifts had to change over, doing the books and ordering stuff. My mom worked in the shop during the day. It was my mom that thought of giving free coffee to the police and traffic cops. Joseph and his wife's little secluded garage was never robbed. The traffic department controlled the traffic to the cemetery when my mom was laid to rest. What a stupid saying: "Laid to Rest" or "Rest in Peace". "Rest in Pieces" will be better. The queue with my mom's funeral was from here to kingdom come – LOL.

Chapter 34

My sister is the youngest of the three older children and she treated me like an older sister should, I would assume. She was always soft and caring but she and her family emigrated from South Africa to Australia and she could not attend the funeral. It must have been very difficult for her. She was very close to my mother and my dad's favourite. I always knew that if I should have a daughter she would be my favourite. I would have liked my daughter to be like my sister.

My sister Marie is very arty; arty farty is how Jonathan and Joseph mocked her but she didn't mind. She loved all three of us the same but felt sorry for me because I was much younger than my two brothers. She was a pretty girl and the best daughter ever to my parents, I am sure. She and her family left for Australia on my mother's birthday. My mother's birthday is the day after Christmas. My mother died less than a year after my sister and her family emigrated.

Marie's real names are Maria Magdalena, but she was already Marie by the time that I was born. Jonathan stayed Jonathan and Joseph stayed Joseph. Johnathan never became John and Joseph never Joe or even Jo without the 'e'. I however often became Jim or worse, Jimmy.

My mother's funeral was three days later and I was one of the carriers of the coffin. A beautiful polished light oak coffin with chrome plated hard plastic handles. A massive arrangement of white flowers was on top of the coffin as it was lowered into the ground. The sun was beating down and everybody was in a hurry to get back under the shade.

My mother's friend, Riaan was the minister that conducted both the service in church and had the last word at the graveside. He did not speak to the people gathered there. He spoke directly to my mom in the coffin as if he could see her. As if he was speaking to a real living person standing in front of him.

I also gave the police and traffic cops coffee when I was manning the shop at night. Then I started giving packets of cigarettes to them as well. It got out of hand and Joseph had to put a stop to it. I am sure there will be no traffic cops manning the streets when I start "Resting in Pieces".

The neighbours in the apartment next to us phoned Jonathan that night or rather phoned him in the early morning. It was only me in the apartment. It has only been me since my mom died. I was laying on the carpet in front of the TV in the lounge and was making strange noises. I was in the foetal position and I was howling to the unseen moon. It scared the neighbours. It scared the living daylights out of them and I had to be moved. I guess "transported off" would have been preferable to all present. I was a casualty of collateral damage. That sounds good. Sounds as if I had a purpose. As if I had a roll. As if I was in a stage show. As if my whole life was a show: enter left exit right. Some people play for the audience, some for themselves. Some are controlled by the voice in their head. It was time for me to exit.

I will never ever be able to comprehend Freud's sexual fascination with his mother.

Chapter 35

What an exit. I was dumped at my mother's friend, Riaan's shelter for the washed-up or is it washed-outs? Preacher Riaan was a lay preacher with many talents that knew a lot of people and their inner most secrets. Even my voice had quieten down, as if part of it has died with my mother.

Me, I was trapped. I was a gold fish in a glass bowl shaped like a rondavel. I was the flickering moon shadows on the rondavel wall with no means of communicating. I had become Simon talking to the pig's head but I wasn't hallucinating. I had the answer but have missed the opportunity. I was surviving from day to day, living for the odd Sunday. I had a song but couldn't sing it. I could empathize with the long ago inmates of the Magdalene Laundries in Ireland. Imagine, God is great from a distance. My mom used to say "The path to hell is paved with good intentions".

The shelter was an old gold mine mansion built when gold was first discovered on the Witwatersrand. It had many rooms but we were not allowed into it during the day. We had to earn our keep. We were dropped in town to collect money for the shelter. The hours and hours in the African sun turned my skin to leather. Some collectors would disappear after a good day's takings with a full collection tin just to come back days or weeks later. They were not always allowed back so where was I to go? I had nowhere.

The shelter was miles from everywhere in the middle of nowhere, surrounded by sterile washed out soil. Nothing grew on the old mine dumps once the gold was extracted. The gold was extracted using cyanide.

The shelter was a gift from the mining company listed on the JSE stock exchange. A peace offering to the people to justify the raping of the land. It was not worth anything without the god given natural resources. One could not even farm the land. It was capitalism in its rawest form but people were grateful. Riaan would have more than one sermon every Sunday and visitors were allowed. Visitors were taken on a tour through the facilities. Were shown the neatly made beds in the rooms, the clean bathrooms, the damaged tins that certain individuals have forced open to buy water while collecting at the traffic lights. Or to buy beer or drugs just to come crawling back.

Visitors were shown the fully stocked rows and rows of freezers in the cellar. Freezers and shelves overflowing with food donated by upmarket supermarkets and grocery stores. The dates on the packages just touching their use by dates. The visitors left the grand old now practical mansion more than just a little bit impressed. They left with their hearts full and their spirits lifted. Some stayed for the second service and a second collection.

It is all in the presentation.

Chapter last

The shade under the green tree was cool and I was sitting comfortably, even though the newly turned soil was slightly moist; not from rain but from the garden team watering the trees and flowers and even the dusty lawn for the few visitors that may or may not turn up during visiting hours on a Sunday afternoon between services. One never knows – the universe has its own momentum.

I only wore a tie on Sundays and not every Sunday. Only those Sundays that my dad would visit to go with me to the little church on the barbed wire fenced grounds of the place that I have now called home for nearly a year. The place that I was committed to at age thirty with no future, no past. A shared room void of any personal possessions. A room that was out of bounds during the day.

I saw myself taking two hands of sand. I was running it through my fingers. Again and again. First slowly and then faster. I was hypnotised by it. Scoop it up in both hands and let it run out through my fingers. Grains of sand timed to fall without touching, two hands of sand that fall and mix without changing the sequence of a single grain. Two solar systems, two universe... until everything fits into everything without touching.

There is no glamour in death even though we glorify it. The body starts decomposing as the electrons slow down; when the nucleus finally loses its hold with the last breath. Leonardo da Vinci knew that. He was intrigued by it; he risked his life for it. He dissected human corpses at a time when it was a serious criminal offence, just to try and understand it.

There was not a sound to be heard; not even a bird or a bee. No butterflies, nothing. No future, no past. I had run out of sand. The sun was shining and I was at total peace as I reached back across the ages.

My dad was lonely after my mom passed away. The tree was standing barely as high as me but with strong branches. I did not have to get up to tie the other end of the tie around the strongest branch. I just had to lift my slightly damp bum a few inches to reach it. The voice went quiet.

I pray that someone is still thinking about my Daddy. That someone somewhere still remembers his name.

A story for Dorothy.

Cuddle me.

Chapter One:

I don't know whether it was the lightning or the thunder that woke me. I realized that the storm must be right above when the second flash was immediately followed by the deep stomach roll of thunder that shook the window frames. I became aware of the car alarm as I reached out for the empty space next to me in our queen size bed. A lonely dog was barking in the distance. The bark was coming from the same general direction as the cock that we could hear most mornings; the country bliss of staying in a small village, but still less than thirty miles from the center of Belfast. There was no going back to sleep now. Not with all the thoughts that were just there as the storm moved off towards the west, Newcastle in Northern Ireland way.

I liked the cold kitchen tiles under my bare feet.

I have been more aware of my feet ever since my diabetes was confirmed just over a year ago but I have always walked around with no shoes on in the house.

I didn't switch the light on. It was light enough in the kitchen now that the skies have cleared even though I could still see streaks of lighting over the horizon to the left. I have stopped closing the blinds last thing at night before going to bed since she is not around anymore.

I had no real appetite but picked at some of the leftover sandwiches from the funeral two days ago. Whatever is not eaten today will have to be thrown out, just in time for the blue bin that will be emptied this morning.

The oven clock was blinking 04:10 in the semi-darkness as the kettle started boiling: Exactly ten days and ten minutes since I have pressed the big continental pillow down onto her face.

Chapter Two:

My silent tears were dripping into her slightly open month as I finally lifted the oversized pillow. There was no breath pushing back to slow the trickle of my warm tears. Her eyes were staring into mine. Both of us were not registering anything. It felt as if time has stopped breathing as well.

I have seen dead people before and knew that her muscles would soon start relaxing. This will return some of her former healthy beauty.

I was at total peace for the first time in six weeks as I rolled off my knees that were planted either side of her and back into bed next to her. It was not yet time to dial 999. The next few hours were mine. And hers.

I cradled her onto my arm and pulled the duvet back over both of us with my left hand. There was still some warmth left in her body as I slowly traced and retraced her face with my index finger: Round and around, peeping into the one window, then the next, finally to knock on the door waiting for her to open her mouth, a game of discovery that I used to play many years ago with my own children.

She and I had no children of our own.

My tears didn't stop and I didn't care. It was as if I have finally moved onto another level, onto an emotional plane unlike anything that I have ever experienced. I felt godlike or at least, I felt in total harmony with the universe. As if I my chest would burst from the fresh air that seemed to have flooded into our room now that there was only one person breathing it.

It was close on seven o'clock when I lifted the phone and dialed 999.

Chapter Three:

I had to smile when I stopped in front of her house.

The directions scribbled onto the no longer white paper serviette, was clear, the house itself could have been lifted from the drawing of a seven year old deep in concentration:

Blocked square, with a pitched roof and chimney to the right, a red door with a window on either side, framed by red shutters, and a smiling walk up to the front door.

All that was missing were curly white smoke from the chimney, a triangular orange face sun hanging in the left top corner and a white cotton cloud.

We easily settled into a contended routine: I cancelled the garden services and started cutting the grass every Friday. She put an extra plate on the table.

Weekends, when at home, normally included a thirty five minute drive to Newcastle where we would park in the first available space for a hand-in-hand walk with no defined purpose or timeline. It became a familiar game of follow-the-leader that always ended at our bench facing the ocean.

We sometimes had to wait, pretending that we were looking out over the cold water, while waiting for the bench to become available. But we never left without sitting down where I could not resist but would lean over and kiss her open mouth swallowing her laugh. She the pretend shy one in public would blush and look away just to reach out and squeeze my hand always available where I picked up the paper wrapped nougat on that first Sunday. The wonder of her never ceased to surprise me.

Chapter Four:

There was a fresh bite in the breeze from the sea when I sat down on the wooden bench in front the four Star Slieve Donard Hotel in Newcastle Northern Ireland.

The hotel was behind me, the view to die for and it was quiet. Most of the guests were either still sleeping or having breakfast.

I was only vaguely aware of her as she sat down. The morning breeze was cool but the sun was above the hotel and starting to warm the back of my neck. I was at peace with the world as I reached out and picked up the small bar of chocolate that I took from the fridge in the room.

Something was wrong. It was only after the second bite that I realized that it didn't taste like chocolate. It was way too sweet for my taste. She was looking at the pink and white nougat in my hand, a smile in her eyes. I dropped my eyes and became aware of her not too small cleavage. It was my turn to turn pink.

We walked back to the hotel a few hours later. My neck was red from the sun.

I did not sleep in my room that night. Neither of us had any sleep that night.

We trekked to the top of Slieve Donard the next Saturday. I could not help but remark about the similarity between the silhouette of the rocks left in a pile on the top of the highest mountain in Northern Ireland and what I saw that first time when she leaned forward on the wooden bench to teasingly help herself to my bar of chocolates.

Chapter Five:

We got married six months later in Spain, just the two of us.

That is the way that we both wanted it.

Her friends quickly became my friends and my somewhat smaller circle of mainly work colleagues, quickly accepted her but we wanted to be alone.

The translator did not turn up for the official ceremony but we persuaded the official with his bandolier across his shoulder and chest to proceed even though we did not understand a word of Spanish. We were giggling like teenagers when we finally signed the register.

We had a meal with champagne before walking back to our hotel. I had to support her. She had most of the champagne and I have never been happier in my 55 years. It was ten days of sun and sea... It didn't stop once we were back at home. It never subsided over the next four years. Not even after she got sick.

Chapter Six:

She never complained, never, not once.

She was my sanity when I wanted to fight the unseen, to scream at the non-caring world.

There was no answer.

We would stay awake at night, lying in bed, with the window open, talking.

The rest of the world slowly withdrew until it was just us two.

She decided to stop all treatment.

She didn't fear dying but for death itself.

It was not necessary to discuss it.

Chapter Seven:

The house was clean and the bed freshly made. I did not go back to it after the second cup of coffee but emptied all the trays and leftover snacks into a black bin bag. I did not touch the sympathy cards on the mantelpiece above the fireplace that she used to light it even when it wasn't really warranted, purely for the atmosphere while we would curl up reading or watching something mindless on TV. Her presence within easy touch all that I wanted.

The black bag was in the blue wheelie bin, ready for our two weekly collection well ahead of time.

I have barely finished showering when the doorbell rang.

It was the nurse that I first met when I was initially diagnosed with diabetes.

Her timing was perfect.

She closed and locked the red door behind her before reaching for my hand. I took it without hesitation, turned around and lead the way up the stairs back to our bedroom.

Sometimes words are not necessary.

Acknowledgements

I have to thank Cara Cunningham who took time out of her weekend in Wales to read my first draft and my wife Linda who is my biggest (and maybe only) fan. I love you lots!

"From a Distance" became a 2011 charity single in support of Magdalene Survivors Together, a charity set in July 2009 by Steven O'Riordan and Gerard Boland focusing on the human rights aspect of the Magdalene Laundries in Ireland.

Steven O' Riordan, was a young Irish filmmaker who had directed and produced a documentary called *The Forgotten Maggies.* It was about the Magdalene Laundries asylum institutions in Ireland.

"From A Distance"

From a distance the world looks blue and green,
and the snow-capped mountains white.
From a distance the ocean meets the stream,
and the eagle takes to flight.

From a distance, there is harmony,
and it echoes through the land.
It's the voice of hope, it's the voice of peace,
it's the voice of every man.

From a distance we all have enough,
and no one is in need.
And there are no guns, no bombs, and no disease,
no hungry mouths to feed.

From a distance we are instruments
marching in a common band.
Playing songs of hope, playing songs of peace.
They're the songs of every man.
God is watching us. God is watching us.

God is watching us from a distance.

From a distance you look like my friend,
even though we are at war.
From a distance I just cannot comprehend
what all this fighting is for.

From a distance there is harmony,
and it echoes through the land.
And it's the hope of hopes, it's the love of loves,
it's the heart of every man.

It's the hope of hopes, it's the love of loves.
This is the song of every man.
And God is watching us, God is watching us,
God is watching us from a distance.
Oh, God is watching us, God is watching.
God is watching us from a distance.

How sad is that?

31037559R00065

Printed in Poland
by Amazon Fulfillment
Poland Sp. z o.o., Wrocław